ADVENT MOMENTS

ADVENT

MOMENTS

*Preparing Your Heart
for the Coming King*

C. NEIL STRAIT   STAN TOLER

Beacon Hill Press of Kansas City
Kansas City, Missouri

Copyright 2000
by Beacon Hill Press of Kansas City

ISBN 083-411-7983

Printed in the
United States of America

Cover Design: Kevin Williamson

Library of Congress Cataloging-in-Publication Data

Strait, C. Neil
    Advent moments : preparing your heart for the coming King / C. Neil
    Strait, Stan Toler.
       p. cm.
    Includes bibliographical references (p.).
    ISBN 0-8341-1798-3 (pb)
       1. Advent—Prayer-books and devotions—English. 2. Christmas—
Prayer-books and devotions—English. 3. Christmas—Meditations. [1. Advent—Meditations.] I. Toler, Stan. II. Title.

BV40 .S76 2000
242'.332—dc21

                                                00-034221

10   9   8   7   6   5   4   3   2   1

Contents

Preface

An exciting part of the Christian year is Advent. Not only is it the promise of gifts and gaiety, but it's the time when deep joy prevails and the great words of spiritual truth—such as "hope," "peace," and "love" —are in the air.

Advent brings us to focus on Jesus, and that's always positive. It confronts us with trust, promise keeping, and obedience. All are events and experiences our hearts need to touch again.

Advent is a lot happening in a short time. In a fast-paced world, we can miss it, move through its days, and be untouched by its beauty and promise. It comes with anticipation but is so many times gone with disappointment—disappointment that we didn't stop to savor its meaning and grasp its hope.

The devotional thoughts in this short book invite you to walk through the Advent days a little more slowly, to hear a word from Scripture, and to let your heart enjoy a journey to Bethlehem—and to Jesus.

May this Advent be a bit clearer, more joyful and richer, not because of what we've written—but because of Jesus.

We pray that rich and lasting "Advent moments" will be yours as you read His story and open your hearts to His Lordship.

Day 1

MATTHEW 1:1—
"A record of the genealogy of Jesus Christ."

History . . . people . . . events . . . births . . . fathers . . . mothers . . . all are the ingredients of the life of Jesus.

While it seems a rather odd way to begin a chapter in the greatest Book ever written, the Savior's earthly genealogy establishes one thing right up front—God and Jesus identify with people.

If the gospel is about anything, it's about people—their value, their dreams, their sorrows, their significance.

Not all on the list are superstars or heroes. When God forms His list, He has classifications different from those we use, particularly love and grace.

What does this mean to a 21st-century person? Plenty. When the success we seek doesn't come, or the promotion goes to another, we're still on His list, in the same place of honor and value. Circumstances and events don't change our value with Him, even when the hard knocks dent our self-image and send us reeling.

The next time you feel left out, let down, drained, discouraged, or depressed, read Matt. 1:1. Keep expanding the list across the centuries. Bring it up to date—and there you are! You're on His list—significant, loved, valued, and graced by His care. He never purges that list. You never drop from His love. Treasure the moment—and the list. Thanks, Matthew!

PRAYER: *Lord, often we wonder where we are in Your care. But Matthew reminds us that we're where we have been—on Your list, next to Your heart, being graced by Your love. Thank You, Father, for knowing where we are even when we forget. In Jesus' name we pray. Amen.*

THINK ABOUT THIS: God's love has no delete key. Everyone on His list gets His love, His care, and His blessings—and so much more!

—*C. Neil Strait*

Thus we can always know that men could live with goodwill and understanding for each other, because one day in each year the little divine Prince of Peace still compels them to do it.

—Charles Jeremiah Wells

Tho' Christ a thousand times
In Bethlehem be born,
If He's not born in thee,
Thy soul is still forlorn.

—Angelus Silesius

That there was no room in the inn was symbolic of what was to happen to Jesus. The only place there was room for Him was on the Cross.

—William Barclay

The hinge of history is on the door of a Bethlehem stable.

—Ralph W. Sockman

Day 2

MATTHEW 1:16—
**"And Jacob the father of Joseph,
the husband of Mary, of whom was
born Jesus, who is called Christ."**

Everyone is identified somehow, by an event, an experience, a mission. "The husband of Mary" says it all—obedience, trust, respect.

Some need few words to describe them. Joseph was such a man. Did he understand all that was happening? No. Did he trust? Yes. Because of his confidence in God's plan, all have been blessed. And because he trusted, obeyed, and respected God's plan, the remainder of the verse was possible—"the husband of Mary, of whom was born Jesus, who is called Christ."

We know so little about Joseph. But what we do know is enough. Some write their lives on the ledgers of time in bold letters. Some write in small caps, but they write deeply. Some let God be large in their lives through simple obedience.

The Josephs are the remembered—not because of what they did, or even how. They don't think how history will record their accomplishments. They think only of obedience, and a world remembers, forever.

Yes, "the husband of Mary." But in that phrase is hidden the link to it all. Without Joseph and his obedience, how would it have been different? God always has a plan, but every plan runs through some Joseph, some obedient heart, someone willing to trust. And where obedience stops, God must find another way, another Joseph.

Our mission first is not to draw the plan or seek success. It's to know God's plan, submit in obedience, and let Him write the history.

PRAYER: *Father, we're so success-driven in our world, and so little of the success that comes seems to enrich us. May we seek first Your will. Teach us to have obedient hearts.*

THINK ABOUT THIS: God's plans come through our hearts never to inhibit us but to enrich us—and others.

—*C. Neil Strait*

The time draws near the birth of Christ:
The moon is hid; the night
is still;
The Christmas bells from
hill to hill
Answer each other in the mist.

—Alfred, Lord Tennyson

The feet of the humblest may walk in the fields
Where the feet of the holiest have trod.
This, this is the marvel to mortals revealed,
When the silvery trumpets of Christmas have pealed,
That mankind are the children of God.

—Phillips Brooks

Today in the town of David a Savior has been born to you; he is Christ the Lord.

—Luke 2:11

Day 3

MATTHEW 1:16—
"And Jacob, the father of Joseph,
the husband of Mary, of whom was
born Jesus, who is called Christ."

"Mary, of whom was born Jesus." This doesn't tell the whole story. What about the fears? The unknown? Or simply the magnitude of this birth? What must have been the thoughts in this young girl's mind?

God sometimes steps out of the ordinary to do the extraordinary. Surely this was such a moment. Here is an unknown girl—a teenager—entrusted with God's special gift. Here is excitement mixed with fear, wonder mixed with questions, hope mixed with humanness.

What were Mary's unrecorded questions or the depths of her fears? What persuaded Mary to trust? What traveled through her mind on that Bethlehem night? We have no way of knowing.

But one ingredient needs to be added—God. The Heavenly Father shared His secret with Mary. An angel shared with Joseph, who surely shared with Mary. God does not use humanity to do His will without revelation and purpose. His will unfolds through a relationship—a relationship of trust.

God spoke words of comfort and counsel to Mary. Luke 2:19 tells us, "Mary treasured up all these things and pondered them in her heart."

Mary was apparently more comfortable with her relationship with God than she was with whatever fears accompanied her mission. So why are we surprised? Relationships should naturally build trust, especially a relationship with the God of creation.

Advent is a lesson in trust at its deepest level—for Joseph, for Mary, for us. And trust is what our relationship with God needs if we're to be lifted above the fears and questions that surround us.

PRAYER: *Eternal God, so much of life haunts us and leaves us with unanswered questions. Teach us the way of trust—a trust that calms our fears and sets our spirits free to walk in obedience to You.*

THINK ON THIS: Joseph and Mary didn't have to find neat answers for their Bethlehem experience. Instead, they had God, whom they trusted. And somehow, in the silent moments when fears speak the loudest, Joseph and Mary were at peace. They had found the Peace-Giver.

—*C. Neil Strait*

Day 4

LUKE 1:28—
"The Lord is with you."

Aren't you afraid?" her daddy said to the little girl as they walked past a dark forest. "Maybe there's a lion or tiger in there," he said jokingly as he pointed to the shadowy row of trees.

"Daddy!" the little girl responded as she walked hand in hand with her father, "stop teasin'. You know I'm not afraid!"

"And why not?" her daddy replied.

"Well, 'cause, you know—I have part of your hand, but you have all of mine!"

The angel made the announcement to Mary that would forever alter her life: "You will be with child and give birth to a son." Everything from that moment on would be a maze of uncertainty. She was walking past the dark forest of the unknown.

Would her friends and family forsake her?

Who would take her in after everyone turned from her?

How would she face the ridicule of her society?

How would she support herself now?

Who could she depend upon?

Heaven prefaced the announcement with a promise: "The Lord is with you." From the beginning of those events that would change history, the Everlasting Father had a firm hand on all of it. Mary knew she would be walking down a very strange path. Everything and everyone she depended upon would soon drift away like windblown sands. But her Father knew she wouldn't walk alone.

Joshua heard a similar word one day as he faced the loneliness of a life without his friend and mentor, Moses. "Do not be terrified; do not be discouraged, for the LORD your God will be with you wherever you go" (Josh. 1:9).

He wouldn't be the last to understand that promise. Generations have come and gone. Pilgrim travelers in each of those generations have trekked past their own dark forests.

We've walked shivering in the cold rains of death and separation. We've felt the hostile winds of misunderstanding beat against our frame. We've held lightly to the hand of the Father. Yet the one thread that wove itself through their pilgrim garments, the one thing that held them—holds us—is the everlasting promise: "The Lord is with you."

Christmas is a promise that flies in the face of our unknowns. The Lord is with us and has all of our hand in His. We can trust Him.

PRAYER: *Father, help us understand what a firm grasp You have on us. We know we'll walk past "dark forests," but help us to fully understand that we'll never walk alone. In Jesus' name. Amen.*

THINK ABOUT THIS: Our unknowns are well known to our Heavenly Father.

—*Stan Toler*

Day 5

LUKE 1:30—
"Do not be afraid, Mary, you have found favor with God."

Mary was an unlikely candidate for such a noble assignment.

Her age.

Her frailty.

Her innocence.

Her reputation.

None of it seemed to make sense in the light of heaven's next words: "You have found favor with God."

Mary, a resident of Nazareth, was unknown by the human race apart from her family and her circle of friends. That would soon change. All of her adolescent struggles to fit in, all of her future standing in the community, all of her dreams of normalcy—she would risk everything to gain God's acceptance.

She would later question the Advent announcements. "How will this be . . . since I am a virgin?" (v. 34). Perhaps she was saying, "I don't understand— why, of all people, did you choose me?" Her tender heart would soon know the topic of the tongue waggers. Perhaps she had felt their barbs before, in tiny scenes of adolescent bumbling. But this would be far different. She would have to risk the rejection of those she loved and respected.

Yet, in her submission to the divine plan, she would gain a belonging that she had never known before. She would fall out of favor with many. But she would gain acceptance by the One who mattered most—her Heavenly Father.

"Mary, you have found favor with God."

Kings would trade their titles for such acceptance. Fortune seekers would barter their goods to buy such an eternal assurance.

Years later, the pen of a white-haired servant exiled to the isle of Patmos would write with amazement of such acceptance: "How great is the love the Father has lavished on us, that we should be called children of God!" (I John 3:I).

We, who have known failure, we, who have been frail when we should have been strong—*we* belong to God. *We* have found His favor.

And we know that our acceptance was not of our doing, but all His. His royal blood flows miraculously through our veins from the moment we risk our own reputation to follow Him.

It all began with a young teen who would dare to risk her past and her future for the realization of God's acceptance.

PRAYER: *Lord, give me the courage to risk everything for Your acceptance. Help me to know that if I belong to You, I truly belong. Help me not to seek for acceptance in worldly relationships or causes if it means knowing less of You. In Jesus' name. Amen.*

THINK ABOUT THIS: Though God loves the whole world, He does have favorites. His Son was born to create a family of believers who would belong exclusively to Him through His death on a Cross.

—*Stan Toler*

Day 6

LUKE 1:37—
"Nothing is impossible with God."

D addy, God's everywhere, isn't He?" the little boy asked.

"Yes, Son—God's everywhere," his father replied.

"We can't see God, can we?"

"No, Son—we can't see God," the father responded.

"Well, Daddy," the boy continued, "If God's everywhere, and we can't see Him, then how come we don't bump into Him?"

Advent is bumping into God.

He stepped over the impossible barriers of eternity and walked among finite hearts longing to know more about Him. He made the impossibilities of a relationship with himself a wonderful possibility. He bridged the impossible chasm of infinity that separated the created from their Creator, with His most precious treasure—His own Son.

The angel announced to Mary, "The Holy Spirit will come upon you, and the power of the Most High will overshadow you. So the holy one to be born will be called the Son of God" (Luke 1:35).

Skeptics doubt that design. Scoffers laugh at that promise. But even those who question His origin number their years from the pivotal point of His birth.

Nothing will keep Him from us. He walks where we are. Even when He seems far away, we're constantly bumping into Him.

Charles Spurgeon wrote, "When you have no helpers, see all your helpers in God. When you have many helpers, see God in all your helpers. When you have nothing but God, see all in God; when you have everything, see God in everything."[1]

The apostle Peter reminds us, "Though you have not seen him, you love him; and even though you do not see him now, you believe in him and are filled with an inexpressible and glorious joy" (1 Pet. 1:8).

PRAYER: *Thank You, Lord, for the comfort of Your presence. Thank You for the message of Christmas. Help me to understand that Jesus was born to be my dearest Friend.*

THINK ABOUT THIS: We can't go anywhere that God hasn't already inhabited. He's already at *that place* where I'll need Him most.

—*Stan Toler*

Day 7

LUKE 1:38—
"I am the Lord's servant."

It's a Christmas nightmare. The paper has been torn with fury from the gift boxes. Recycled bows litter the family room floor like fallen flowers. Dad is trying desperately to insert batteries into a just-opened toy. And one child, standing ankle deep in decorations, suddenly asks, "Is this all there is?"

Mom blushes in shame while the other siblings shake their heads in disbelief. It's an all-too-familiar scene.

Advent is all about giving—not about getting. It's about putting self aside long enough to respond to a Savior. Bethlehem's First Family had a heart of obedience to the will of the Father. Every move was motivated by their allegiance to Him. Whatever it cost, wherever it led—doing the will of God was all that mattered.

A servant is without options. Servanthood is surrender to the Lordship of the Master.

It was for Mary. In the face of the unknown—and the known—she was able to say to the announcing angel, "May it be to me as you have said."

A missionary translator was struggling to find a way to translate the New Testament word "obedience." Taking a break from his work one day, he went outside and whistled for his dog. The pet came running at full speed. The translator's native assistant commented, "Your dog is all ears." Immediately the missionary knew he had the translation he needed. Obedience is being all ears.

The true spiritual worship of Advent is to be all ears to the message and to the Messenger. Like Samuel of old, we whisper, "Speak, for your servant is listening" (I Sam. 3:10).

We will need to make a determined effort to hear the Lord's voice above the confusing sounds of the season. We will need to listen to His words of love and acceptance. We will need to listen, to hear Him call us by name even in the midst of a crowded store. We will need to bend our ear to the manger and hear heaven say, "This was for you."

And we will rise to do the will of One of whom it was said, "Being found in appearance as a man, he humbled himself and became obedient to death" (Phil. 2:8).

PRAYER: *Lord, help me not to be a slave to the season. Help me to rediscover a servant's heart. I want to surrender to Your will, not to the will of retailers and advertisers. My heart's desire is to be Your servant. In Jesus' name I pray. Amen.*

THINK ABOUT THIS: True servants of Christ are the only persons who are truly free.

—*Stan Toler*

Day 8

MATTHEW 1:18—
**"She was found to be with child
through the Holy Spirit."**

What a privilege to have an entry in the eternal record naming you the mother of Jesus by the Holy Spirit! While the sages and theologians dissect it, debate it, and doubt it, there is one who knows the truth—Mary.

History has a way of wrapping its reality around the truth. If that truth and that event involve a teenage girl named Mary, so be it. History records the facts and leaves the wonder and questions for others to figure out.

But God is the Maker of history—especially incarnation history. This is His domain. He supplies the person, the plan, the place, and drops His Son into history in a way totally unimaginable to human thought. The Holy Spirit, Jesus, and Mary etch an event in history that forever changes human destiny.

When age by age the story comes back, Joseph and Mary are reviewed once again. The same questions surface, the same wonders are there, and the incarnate Christ is considered. But at the center of it all is an unknown teenage girl, Mary.

It's a well-known fact that often the great births are but silent footnotes in history, and the changing tides sweep the shores as if nothing has happened. Then comes reality—a person, an experience, an event—and the future beats with excitement. It's all incarnation wonder, God invading our hearts and spreading His glorious banner of hope.

God chooses strangely sometimes, and Mary is a case in point. But her name, her memory, her trust, and her obedience are forever written in the early chapters of the redemption story. They invite us to a journey—to Bethlehem, Calvary, and an empty tomb. Ultimately we're set free, redeemed, and the Light of Bethlehem makes sense of God's strange choices.

PRAYER: *O God of love, I want to be set free by the love that stirred Mary and birthed Your Son. I want what You brought to our world by Bethlehem's wonder. May I trust You with my questions and welcome You to be my Redeemer and Sanctifier.*

THINK ON THIS: Mary is only a name, like any other name, until trust and obedience began writing God's story in her life and in His world. Then it's not just Mary—it's Mary, the mother of Jesus.

—*C. Neil Strait*

Day 9

MATTHEW 1:19—
"Because Joseph her husband
was a righteous man."

One word says it all. If you can choose only one word to describe Joseph, "righteous" is a good one.

"Righteous" says nothing about career but everything about character. It says nothing about self but worlds about commitment. It says nothing about Joseph's desire to seal his fame in the Bethlehem story, but it says all God needed to know about Joseph to give him a lead part in the Advent drama.

What qualifies you and me for the drama God is planning? What bottom-line information does one need? Stats and stature? No. One word: "righteous."

It's a word that explains the past, identifies the present, and predicts the future. "Righteous" is all you need to know. God saw this humble man's righteous heart and staged one of His greatest events on that one reality.

Maybe more work on being righteous and less on recognition is the message Advent brings to us. Joseph was so intent on preserving the respect for Mary that he was willing to take the hit for her pregnancy. But then God steps in. "An angel of the Lord appeared to him . . . and said . . . do not be afraid" (Matt. 1:20).

A righteous life has the attention and care of God. He found in Joseph the one thing He needed to complement the Son He was bringing to Bethlehem —"a righteous man."

PRAYER: *Father, teach us the way of righteousness, for it's the fountain piece of all that's right and good. May we long for it, hunger for it, for we know that nothing will nurture life like the ways of righteousness.*

THINK ON THIS: If righteousness is what God honors, why do we spend time and energy and life seeking so many other things?

—*C. Neil Strait*

This is Christmas: not the tinsel, not the giving and receiving, not even the carols, but the humble heart that receives anew the wondrous gift, the Christ.

—Frank McKibben

In the sixth month, God sent the angel Gabriel to Nazareth, a town in Galilee, to a virgin pledged to be married to a man named Joseph, a descendant of David. The virgin's name was Mary.

The angel went to her and said, "Greetings, you who are highly favored! The Lord is with you."

Mary was greatly troubled at his words and wondered what kind of greeting this might be.

But the angel said to her, "Do not be afraid, Mary, you have found favor with God.

You will be with child and give birth to a son, and you are to give him the name Jesus."

—Luke 1:26-31

Day 10

MATTHEW 1:20—
"He had in mind to divorce her quietly."

What are the fruits of righteousness? Just as an attitude or an act will produce consequences —either good or bad—so will spiritual attitudes and acts. Righteousness produces good consequences.

For Joseph it led him to consider the right way to respond to Mary's pregnancy. We're back to the age-old but ever-new question, "What would Jesus do?"

Righteousness asks the right questions and gets the right answers. This is true because righteousness is an attribute of God that He shares with His children. Joseph "considered" Mary's plight. But because he was righteous, he had divine counsel. Have we recently considered the privileges of righteous living?

We tend to forget that righteousness is the blessing of relationship with God, and all its consequences are good and right—not always convenient, comfortable, or understood, but in the long term always good and right.

Whomever you serve, whatever path you take in life, it will bear consequences—some good, some bad. Some consequences are predictable. Sin will always render sad and tragic consequences in time. Righteousness produces good consequences. The facts of both are not determined by human laws or judgments, but by a God who created with wisdom and intent.

Advent has the fruits of righteousness written all over it. Bethlehem is one of the many good consequences of righteousness.

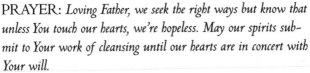

PRAYER: *Loving Father, we seek the right ways but know that unless You touch our hearts, we're hopeless. May our spirits submit to Your work of cleansing until our hearts are in concert with Your will.*

THINK ON THIS: The righteous life asks unselfish questions, the answers of which benefit both self and others.

—*C. Neil Strait*

God rest you merry, gentlemen;
Let nothing you dismay.
Remember Christ, our Savior,
Was born on Christmas day.

—English carol

Christmas began in the heart of God. It is
complete only when it reaches the heart of man.

—Anonymous

Day 11

MATTHEW 1:20—
"Do not be afraid."

God's favorite phrase is "Do not be afraid." This is its first appearance in the New Testament. It's very appropriate and is spoken to Joseph, husband of Mary, at a scary time.

God has a way of sharing His best with us in our worst times. Joseph was perplexed—"A baby? How? Why us? *Mary?*" Questions just come at such times. But questions are put to rest with God's favorite phrase, "Do not be afraid."

Though new to Joseph, the admonition wasn't new with God. From His comfort to Abram in Gen. 15:1, you hear it over 100 times in the Scriptures. God was and is serious about His care and love.

Back to Joseph. Did he argue with God and say, "Easy for *You* to say, God"? Or did he settle into the yoke of God's care and trust this unreasonable, hard-to-understand, scary moment to Him? The answer is in Matt. 1:24: "When Joseph woke up, he did what the angel of the Lord had commanded him and took Mary home as his wife."

Want a lesson in obedience and trust? This one is hard to beat. Trust calls us not in the understood moments of life but at the precise moments. When the future is frightening, when the news is devastating, when life makes no sense, when we would rather run, God invites us to walk and settle into a trust stance. By His words "Do not be afraid," He's asking us to let our weight down on Him, to trust Him, to take our hands off and walk in obedience.

Easy to say, hard to do. God's "Do not be afraid" is an all-occasion command—for every experience, every fear, for every journey. And until you and I hear this word and trust Him in this, God can't do for us what He knows we need and what deep down we want.

So for the uncertain times, let God's favorite phrase be yours—"Do not be afraid."

PRAYER: *Creator God, You know our fears and our future, and You know we need You. Give us trusting spirits and obedient hearts to grasp Your wonderful command "Do not be afraid."*

THINK ON THIS: God doesn't waste words just to get us to the next crisis. He gives us His promise to strengthen us for any and all crises.

—*C. Neil Strait*

Day 12

MATTHEW 1:21—
"You are to give him the name Jesus, because he will save his people from their sins."

The name "Jesus." What does it bring to mind? It encompasses all that's good and right. It ignites hope. It has the sound of love and forgiveness. Everything the name "Jesus" brings to mind is positive. You can't harbor a negative thought when you think of Him.

This Jesus brings to us the things of God—righteousness, goodness, love, joy, peace, holiness, redemption—the list goes on. All these words are positive, uplifting, hope-filled.

Contrast these to the words describing what He came to save us from—"He will save his people from their sins"—and you get a different picture. Sin conjures up all negatives—disobedience, transgression, selfishness, sorrow, alienation, hatred, hopelessness, to name a few. All are distasteful and reek with despair.

Jesus came with God's best to save us from sin's worst. Jesus came all the way to our sinfulness to salvage us from the ash heap and set our feet on new and better paths.

That's why the name "Jesus" is a joy. It's a reminder of God coming through His Son to give us a better life for today and a brighter hope for tomorrow. Life needs such landmarks of truth and joy to touch those with despairing hearts.

PRAYER: *Eternal and gracious God, we praise You for Your redemptive love that forgave our sins and etched hope on our hearts and future. In Jesus' name we pray. Amen.*

THINK ON THIS: Had Jesus not come to us, life would have forever been in bondage to sin and recipient of the worst.

—*C. Neil Strait*

Day 13

MATTHEW 1:22—
"All this took place to fulfill what the Lord had said through the prophet."

"All this" is hard to comprehend. We're over-whelmed with the little we *do* comprehend.

We're constantly being stretched with "all this" that God does. We marvel at it and rejoice in it. We thank Him for it. And we don't understand half of it.

But that's OK. The part we understand warms the heart. When we need to learn more, God has His way of opening His classroom in our heart and stretching us a little more.

Today's scripture is a reminder that God's "all this" is never the end chapter. There's always more.

For Joseph and Mary, it changed their lives for-ever, and for the better. This is the promise of Advent. God's "all this" is an unfolding, ever-expanding experience. God is forever larger than life, drawing us to Him in creative ways, gracing our lives with new-ness, freshness, and growth. It's God's way to come and be part of life on the human dimension.

So the Advent is ongoing. It's God continuing His love, His plan, His promise. And what it does for us is birth hope and grace in the midst of our despair and trials. He authors a new day and walks with us into a better tomorrow.

PRAYER: *Lord, keep our hearts and minds open to what You want us to learn. There's so much, but may our hearts grasp enough to be joyous on our journey with You.*

THINK ON THIS: In the school of Christ there's no boring subject and no wasted day. He is "fresh every morning," waiting to lead us to higher ground.

—*C. Neil Strait*

Day 14

MATTHEW 1:22—
"All this took place to fulfill what the Lord had said through the prophet."

"All this took place." Reality! It happened! People saw it! History relives it every year. God kept His word.

That God kept His word is not a surprise, though. He's been doing it from the beginning. Christians don't need a Bethlehem to convince them of God's faithfulness. It's scattered along the biblical journey.

Wherever you check in on the biblical record, soon you'll discover a promise made and a promise kept. You'll find faithfulness. It's seen in the lives of God's people, great and small. Faithfulness is the characteristic of God. All who walk with Him can affirm, "He's been faithful to me."

We believe in the Incarnation not because of

the manger, the innkeeper, Mary, or even the Baby. We believe because God kept a covenant with His people. He came as He promised. And in an age when the world is low on trust examples, God's faithfulness is a great encouragement.

Bethlehem is not only a story about Bethlehem, Joseph, Mary, and the Christ—it's also a story of prophecy being fulfilled, another chapter in the story of God's faithfulness. It's about faith, trust, and confidence. We need to drink deeply of these, for they're in such short supply these days.

When we focus more on the character and covenant of God, the events surrounding Bethlehem don't surprise us—they confirm Him! They validate faith and etch hope a little deeper into our hearts.

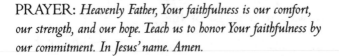

PRAYER: *Heavenly Father, Your faithfulness is our comfort, our strength, and our hope. Teach us to honor Your faithfulness by our commitment. In Jesus' name. Amen.*

THINK ON THIS: God is the only One who has the long history of thousands, maybe millions, of years fulfilling His Word, keeping His promises. He has never defaulted—and never will!

—C. Neil Strait

Heap on more wood!
The wind is chill;
But let it whistle as it will,
Merry still.
　　　—Sir Walter Scott

God came to earth in human form. The impact
of his birth was so great that calendars were torn
up, prejudices were laid aside, and people began
to walk in newness of life.

　　　—Billy Graham

Day 15

MATTHEW 1:22—
"All this took place to fulfill . . ."

God is amazing. With a world to keep track of, made up of too many who do not like His tracking, He's a God of timing, faithfulness, and word-keeping.

Has He ever been late? No. Ever defaulted on a promise? No. Walk through the corridors of history, and what do you find? Faithfulness written on every page. After every journey we take through the tough nights of the soul, our conclusion is "He's been faithful to me."

Advent, you see, is not about a Baby only or a teenage mother or a trusting husband. It's about God coming at just the right time for you and me. "All this took place to fulfill . . ." a word that God had given decades ago. It all took place so you and I could have a Savior.

The fascinating thought about God is His awesome care. A billion things could have His attention. Less than half a dozen foul us up. Yet "all this took place to fulfill what the Lord had said through the prophet" (v. 22).

One of the lessons here is that God sees word-keeping as a priority. Every time we see a rainbow, it serves as a reminder of God's covenant—and His faithfulness.

The Advent of Jesus is a reminder that God is never late. Whatever need or fear or heartbreak you bear, take hope. God will come when it's time. Turn your amazement into acceptance. That's why He came, not to amaze us, but to redeem us, to be invited into our hearts, our needs, our fears.

PRAYER: *Eternal God, may we know more than the facts of Your faithfulness. May we invite You into our hearts to be Savior, and may we live a personal history with You.*

THINK ON THIS: That Jesus came is not a surprise if you know anything about God. That so many have not welcomed Him is the surprise.

—*C. Neil Strait*

The Burning Babe

As I in hoary winter's night stood shivering in the snow,
Surprised I was with sudden heat which made my heart to
glow;
And lifting up a fearful eye to view what fire was near,
A poor Babe all burning bright did in the air appear;
Who, scorched with excessive heat, such floods of tears did
shed,
As though his flood should quench his flames which with his
tears were fed.

—Robert Southwell, 1561

Day 16

MATTHEW 1:23—
"The virgin will be with child."

I don't want to make more of this than I should, but the reference to "the virgin" gets my attention. It identifies a real person. How amazing that of all young women living even at the time of Christ, He chose this one—"the virgin."

Come to think of it, throughout history God's methods of choosing haven't deviated much. Take for instance His choices of Moses, Noah, and Abraham —and many more in the Old Testament.

But fast-forward to today. There are you and me and how many others we know whom God has singled out. We see a father or a mother, a son or daughter, and on it goes—people whom God has personally called to His service, positioned in a strategic place of His unfolding plan.

God's plan to love His world and be Savior to

everyone finally comes down to one person at a time. The virgin at Bethlehem, Paul of the Mediterranean region, a missionary here, a pastor or staff person there, laypeople all over the world . . . the network of His love is individually identified. And where He finds obedience, there He births in them His mission, His plan, and His Spirit.

Bethlehem teaches us that no person is insignificant. The teenage girl, unheard of, finds a place in God's plan. Are you listening? You see, it was not that Mary was so gifted or so extraordinary. She was obedient, had a heart to trust, and was ready to say "yes!" We can do that too.

Obedience, trust, and a ready heart are ingredients of miracles, of Bethlehems, of hope.

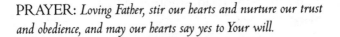

PRAYER: *Loving Father, stir our hearts and nurture our trust and obedience, and may our hearts say yes to Your will.*

THINK ON THIS: God must have a person for all His plans, but He will take only obedient, trusting hearts.

—*C. Neil Strait*

A wealthy Boston family held a christening party after the baptism of their baby. Guests and friends swarmed into their palatial home. Soon the party was in full swing. People were having a wonderful time, enjoying one another, eating, drinking, and being merry. Somebody asked, "By the way, where's the baby?"

Instantly the mother's heart shuddered! In questioning panic, she left the room and rushed into the master bedroom, where she had left her baby asleep in the middle of their large bed. She found the baby dead, smothered by the guests' coats!

Don't let Jesus be smothered by the coats of guests as we busy ourselves running here and there.

—Derl Keefer

Day 17

MATTHEW 1:23—
"'The virgin will be with child and will give birth to a son, and they will call him Immanuel'—which means, 'God with us.'"

Immanuel—"God with us." The Incarnation of the Son of God simply means that God has come all the way down to our hearts, our homes, our situations, our chaos. The sovereign God with humans— that's why the gospel is good news!

God is with us by His choice. Certainly neither our rebellious ways nor our selfish hearts motivated His coming. Neither did our sometimes unlovable attitudes. No, out of pure love, agape love, God has come to be with us.

He is with us to bring all that He is into our lives and into our hearts. With hearts dusty from being away from the Father and with lives disarranged from selfish exploits, He comes into the clutter to be God—hope, life, future!

All that God can be is a glad invitation to hearts that are aware of the fact that what a person puts into life isn't much. The hunger and disappointments make the heart ready for His coming.

It's an incomplete cycle until we can respond, "God with us . . . and we with God."

PRAYER: *Father, may we welcome You into our hearts and into our fears today to learn what it really means to have "God with us."*

THINK ON THIS: "God with us" explodes the myth that God is distant and uncaring. He is with us in our worst, working for something better.

—*C. Neil Strait*

Day 18

MATTHEW 1:23—
"'They will call him Immanuel'—
which means, 'God with us.'"

Let's stay with this verse another day. It's a momentous truth, and the Advent of Jesus Christ was a momentous event. This is where history catches its breath—the truth of "God with us!"

We desperately need a God like this, One who can come into the midst of our lives, both its joys and sorrows, and help us make sense out of both. For many—now and then—were beaten down by the hard things, despairing if things would ever get better and seeing no way they could.

Then God came. He always does. He comes to write hope across our despair and to lead us by love.

If we ever wrap our fears around this thought— "God with us"—it will ignite a revolution of hope. It will give rise to an invitation to God from us to come and dwell among us and in us. It will be our personal encounter. It will no longer be an Advent story, but it will be something lived out in our hearts.

Bethlehem was God coming all the way to our hearts and hurts, to spread His care and grace across our fears, walking with us on a journey of hope.

Yes, all I need to hear of the Bethlehem story is "God with us!" But it also invites us onward to hear God's other truths—to listen, to learn, to journey with the One who is the Light of the world, dispelling darkness and brightening every day. This is when true Advent comes.

PRAYER: *Father of light, open our hearts to the truth of "God with us." May we grasp what it means and live in its reality this day.*

THINK ON THIS: If God is not with us, who is? In our wandering we have not found anyone or anything. Our hope is truly Immanuel—"God with us."

—*C. Neil Strait*

Day 19

LUKE 2:6—
**"While they were there, the time
came for the baby to be born."**

L ocation, location, location," the well-known real
estate adage recommends. It seems like Bethlehem's First Family hadn't passed the Real Estate 101
course.

"There."

The location of Christ's birth is almost beyond
comprehension. Granted, it was exactly where God
intended it—according to biblical prophecy. And
granted, it was the only place in the entire town with
a Vacancy sign on it. Yet it certainly was the least obvious location in which the Lord of the universe was
to take up earthly residence.

Come to think of it, all of us have been there—
to the least obvious place for a child of God to take
residence in. We've known moments of displaced dis-

comfort. We've been in places and situations where we didn't seem to belong. It seemed as if all familiarity was gone and we were suddenly living in a borrowed place.

One of the great wonders of the gospel story is the places where Jesus the Christ chose to dwell. For example, He left the adoring presence of the angels in heaven to borrow a room in Bethany with Lazarus and his family. His body was laid in a borrowed tomb after its removal from a borrowed cross.

But no dwelling better expresses His humility than the place of His birth. Modern princes and kings would be born in palaces. A company of doting physicians, nurses, and attendants would oversee their delivery, while anxious reporters waited to broadcast the arrival to a waiting world. Every corner of their delivery room would be scrubbed and polished for the birth of that royal subject.

But royalty would not be born in such a place. It was a dirty manger cave. Cobwebs filled the nooks and crannies, and bugs crawled across animal droppings toward the manger crib.

"There" the very Son of God chose to dwell. "There" light shone brighter than in the most prestigious delivery room ever built. Not by accident, but by divine appointment.

The One who was acquainted with our sorrow

knew about our lonely dwellings. If we were to reside temporarily or permanently in borrowed "manger" places, He would want us to know He understands.

Someone said it wisely: "Christ was content with a stable when he was born so that we could have a mansion when we die."

PRAYER: *Lord Jesus, I acknowledge that You are with me "there." You stand alongside me in the borrowed places of sorrow, separation, and suffering. Thank You for Your presence. In Your name I pray. Amen.*

THINK ABOUT THIS: Our temporary places help us prepare for our permanent dwelling.

—*Stan Toler*

Day 20

LUKE 2:7—
"She . . . wrapped him in swaddling clothes, and laid him in a manger" (KJV).

An adoring son sent his aged parents a new microwave oven, thinking it would make their life simpler. He was surprised to hear his mother's voice on the phone a few days later.

"Hi, Mom," he responded. "Did you get the microwave?"

"Yes, Son," his mother replied. "Your father and I appreciate it very much."

"Does it work?" the son asked.

"Well, that's why I'm calling. We've tried everything, and we just can't seem to get it to work right. In fact, we can't even set the clock. It just keeps blinking!"

"I'm sorry, Mom," the son sympathized. "Did you read the instruction book in the packing box?"

"Yes, Son—we read the instruction book."

"So what do you think the problem is?"

She replied, "Well, I guess we just needed our son to come along with the gift!"

The infant Jesus was wrapped in the clothes of our humanity. He once was robed in the light of a trillion galaxies. He deserved a royal robe. But He was wrapped in swaddling clothes—our frailty, our sin.

On the night of His birth, His tiny voice startled the animals that shared His birthing room. Years later those cries would be replaced with a strong voice—strong enough to startle the devil during His temptation in the wilderness, strong enough to startle the Roman soldiers when He declared the finished work of Calvary on a cross.

Along the way, His voice would not only startle but also soothe, and it would teach the very wisdom of God from seaside to hillside. God the Father did more than send us an instruction Book. He sent His Son along.

He knew how confusing the laws and rituals could be to people like us. But He also knew how important it was for us to keep those laws and practice those rituals. It was His way of conveying His wisdom and His loving presence to us.

Mercy sent a Son along as a living example. The holiness of God demanded holy living. And to teach holy living, He sent the ultimate Example.

PRAYER: *Lord Jesus, thank You for Your example. We live in a world that has lost its sense of direction. Thank You for showing us the way. We seek a heart of holiness, which only You can give. In Your name we pray. Amen.*

THINK ABOUT THIS: He wore our clothes so that we could one day wear His robes.

—*Stan Toler*

Day 21

LUKE 2:10—
"The angel said to them, 'Do not be afraid.'"

Great missionary statesman Hudson Taylor wrote, "All of God's giants have been weak men who did great things for God because they reckoned on God being with them."[1]

Lowly shepherds were graced with heaven's greatest announcement. As we know nobility, theirs was not such a noble vocation. Though the economy of their times certainly placed great value on them, their only following was sheep.

Yet the angelic announcement passed the palace gate and came to rest over the sand-swept dwelling of a few shepherds. Its very method was a revelation of God's economy. Riches poured on the lowly, salvation shining on the uneducated, streams of grace winding their way through the hearts of the unenlightened and unknown.

They must have been terribly afraid. They were truly "touched by an angel." Their serene surroundings exploded with strange lights and sounds as heaven's messenger spoke the promise of the ages to their unsuspecting hearts.

Fear drove them to their knees. But faith caused them to stand and take notice—and faith drove them from their place of confusion to a house of true worship. Every step was a step of trust in the messenger and the message.

The shepherds taught us much. From our lowly places of confusion and fear, we've learned to see God's awesome salvation and strength. From our uneducated hearts, we've reached out to grasp divine truth. From our finite weakness, we've learned to rest ourselves on the divine.

"Do not be afraid." What a message for these times! Darkness settles over our souls with the covers of night. We go about our menial tasks with no certainty of a tomorrow. And then heaven speaks the message to our spirit: "Do not be afraid. A Savior has been born!"

The truth may pass by the closed doors of the palace. But it will find its way to the trusting, no matter their rank or station.

66

PRAYER: *Father, help us to open our hearts to the announcement of Your presence. Help us to understand that what You have freely given to us we could never afford. We accept by obedient faith. In Jesus' name we pray. Amen.*

THINK ABOUT THIS: Faith believes God in the dark.

—*Stan Toler*

Day 22

LUKE 2:10—
"I bring you good news of great joy that will be for all the people."

It was a nervous moment in the annual church Christmas program. Mother had been coaching Sister for days. The whole family would be there, and it was a wonderful place to show off the little girl's memory skills.

Situated on the front row, Mother waited for the magical moment. Sister arrived on the platform right on cue. The other Sunday School children recited their lines with ease. But the nervous child took one look at the crowd and couldn't remember her own name, let alone the prized few lines.

Mortified, her mom began to whisper the line to her little actress: "I bring you good news of great joy."

With her eyes still frozen on the large crowd,

Sister blurted out, "Mother brings you good news of great joy!"

We're told that nearly 400 million Christmas cards will flow through the mail system during the holidays. None of those cards, however, will ever convey the bright hope of the season any better than a family of believers—believers so filled with the wonder of God's great sacrifice that their hearts spill it spontaneously into every Christmas action.

The myriad activities that have become a part of the Christmas tradition can be permeated with joy. A joyful baking session. A joyful toy construction. A joyful note or letter. A joyful participation in a community outreach. A joyful visit to a shut-in. Each activity may be an action of pure joy.

Christmas joy isn't to be hoarded. It's a message to be shared in love. We can influence our family circle, our circle of friends, our business associates with an attitude of rejoicing, an attitude of thankfulness that God loved us enough to give us His greatest gift—His only Son.

PRAYER: *Father, at this Advent season, let me give Your joy away. Let it fill every activity, let it influence every contact, and let it come from a sanctified and thankful heart. In Jesus' name. Amen.*

THINK ABOUT THIS: Joy is the only gift our friends and family will never want to return.

—*Stan Toler*

Day 23

LUKE 2:11—

"Today in the town of David a Savior has born born to you; he is Christ the Lord."

It has been wisely said: "If our greatest need had been money, God would have sent us an economist; if our greatest need had been pleasure, God would have sent us an entertainer; but our greatest need was forgiveness, so God sent us a Savior."

> Born just in time—"today."
> Born in just the right place—"in the town of David."
> Born for just the right reason—"a Savior has been born to you."

Every single event moved the pieces of the heavenly puzzle to completion. The birth of the Christ child was God's answer to every human problem. The Temple prophet held the infant Jesus in his arms, turned his eyes toward heaven, and proclaimed, "My eyes have seen your salvation" (Luke 2:30).

The story is told of a little boy whose father was killed in World War II. Christmastime was especially hard on the boy, because his friends had their fathers around to share the traditions of the season.

One Christmas morning after the gifts had been unwrapped, the boy went to his mother, gave her a big hug, and thanked her for the presents.

His mom hugged him back and said, "I hope you got everything you wanted for Christmas."

Her son replied, "Well, there *is* one more thing."

"What's that?" Mother replied.

"I wish Dad could be here with us," he answered.

His mother was moved to tears. She walked to the china cabinet, picked up a picture of her husband, and held it to her heart. "Son, I believe your dad is here with us."

"I know that, Mom," the boy said. "I mean I wish Dad could be here so I could give him a big hug and he could hug me back."

The Heavenly Father came to the town of David in the presence of a baby Boy. Now we could *see* salvation. Mary and Joseph hugged God. And God hugged them back. It was a hug we all would share.

Later, God's Son would open His arms of love on a rugged Cross. Salvation's price would be forever settled.

PRAYER: *Father, thank You for salvation's hug. Thank You for forgiveness and acceptance. We want the whole world to see what Your love has done for us through the gift of Your only Son. In Jesus' name. Amen.*

THINK ABOUT THIS: Salvation through faith in the Lord Jesus Christ is the Church's cornerstone. Every other stone has merit only as it relates to that stone.

—*Stan Toler*

Day 24

LUKE 2:12—
"This will be a sign to you: You will find a baby."

Long ago there lived a wise and good king who loved his subjects so much that he wanted to know more about them. He wanted to acquaint himself with how they lived—to know their struggles, their joys, their sorrows. To walk among his people, he would often disguise himself in the common clothes of a working man or even in the rags of a poor man.

Hearing about the hardships of a certain man and his family, the king decided to pay a visit to their home. The family had no idea who was knocking at their door as they opened it to a man dressed like a beggar. They welcomed him in and invited him to have supper with them.

During the conversation at the table, they were impressed with his kindness and compassion as he spoke words of encouragement. He seemed to be deeply moved as they talked about their own challenges. Soon he thanked his host family and left into the night.

The next day the king returned, again as a beggar. "Do you know who I am?" he said.

"Of course," the father replied. "You're the one who shared our meal last evening."

"I am," their guest answered, "but I'm more than that."

"Why, Sir, what do you mean?" the host asked.

The royal guest took off the coat of a beggar to reveal the clothes of royalty underneath. "My friend," he said to the bewildered man, "I came here not just as your guest last night—I came here as your king. I'm *your king!*"

The king was astonished by the father's response: "My lord," he spoke as he knelt before him, "you left the glory of your palace to be with us in our humble home. You ate what the common man eats. You were like one of us. To your other subjects, you have given of your wealth. But to us, O King, you have given your love."

This will be a sign . . . you will find a baby.

He came to the door of our hearts as a Baby to have fellowship with us in the struggles, hurts, and joys of our life.

He could have given us diamonds. But He gave us more—He gave us His love.

PRAYER: *Thank You, Jesus, for coming to our humble home. We've never been the same because of Your visit. In Your name we pray. Amen.*

THINK ABOUT THIS: Sacrificial love demands a sacrificial response.

—*Stan Toler*

Day 25

LUKE 2:14—
**"Glory to God in the highest,
and on earth peace."**

Mother Teresa stood near the podium to receive the acclaimed Nobel Peace Prize. The presenter asked the devout woman who had given her life for the poor of India, "Mother Teresa, what can we do to help promote world peace?"

She answered thoughtfully but with characteristic directness, "Go home and love your family."

Earth was blessed with a magnificent praise concerto on the night Jesus was born. Angelic hosts became the backup singers for heaven's messenger. Theirs was a song of praise aimed at the dreary hearts of a world that had become entangled in the web of religion by laws and ceremonies.

A curious message in song proclaimed the fulfilled promise of "on earth peace."

No more wars? Of course not. The echoing sound of our history has been the sound of gunfire.

No more misunderstanding? Of course not. From Cain and Abel to the latest round of Middle East negotiations, humanity has worn its feelings on its sleeves.

What was the message? Peace has come to earth. Heavenly peace. Lasting peace. Unconditional peace.

We still struggle with its parameters—but we now know where to find it.

Jesus shattered the walls of division that separated Old Testament works from New Testament grace. He crawled across the religious battlegrounds of time with the answer to every question in His heart.

Charles Swindoll in his book *Growing Strong* wrote, "Some gifts you can give this Christmas are beyond monetary value: Mend a quarrel, dismiss suspicion, tell someone 'I love you.' Give something away—anonymously. Forgive someone who has treated you wrong. . . . Give as God gave to you in Christ, without obligation, or announcement, or reservation, or hypocrisy."[1]

Martin Luther sang the message of the angels in his verse:

> *Ah, dearest Jesus, holy Child,*
> *Make Thee a bed, soft, undefiled,*

Within my heart, that it may be
A quiet chamber kept for Thee;

My heart for very joy doth leap,
My lips no more can silence keep,
I too must sing with joyful tongue
That sweetest ancient cradle song.

PRAYER: *Lord, give me a new voice to sing the cradle song.*
And help me to sing it carefully and prayerfully to those around
me. In Your name I pray. Amen.

THINK ABOUT THIS: Peace will not come to our
world unless it first comes to our hearts.

—*Stan Toler*

Day 26

LUKE 2:15—
"Let's go to Bethlehem and see this thing that has happened, which the Lord has told us about."

Radio evangelist M. R. DeHaan once wrote,

> *I'm tired of all this empty celebration,*
> *Of feasting, drinking, recreation;*
> *I'll go instead to Calvary.*
> *And there I'll kneel with those who know*
> *The meaning of that manger low,*
> *And find the Christ—this Christmas.*[1]

Our tendency to focus on the immediate includes the Advent season as well. We fill our to-do lists and carry out our daily plans. The shopping, the trimming, the scheduling, the decorating—all of the immediate duties of Christmas must be accomplished.

But there's a discovery we need to make, a discovery that may halt our busyness. Christ didn't come to earth so that we could have a dinner party. He came to earth to save us from our past, our sins, and give us a hope for the future.

The light of the manger cradle casts a shadow toward the Cross. The true gift of Christmas cost more than anyone could pay. The wages of sin is death. And the vulnerable Infant of Bethlehem would soon be the victorious Savior of Golgotha.

The spiritual discovery of the shepherds began with a resolution—"Let's go to Bethlehem." They had seen the awesome display of that Judean night. They had heard the angelic pronouncements. But there was another discovery to be made. They needed to see Jesus.

Dr. DeHaan said it for us: "There I'll kneel with those who know / The meaning of that manger low."[2] We must make the decision either to remain in spirit with the party crowd or to take a spiritual journey with the chosen few who will seek the Christ.

It takes effort to find Jesus in His birthday celebration. It takes focus. It takes willpower. The discovery is worth the effort. "There" at our spiritual Bethlehem we'll discover a Savior—a Deliverer from all our past and a Friend for all our future.

"So they hurried off and found Mary and Joseph, and the baby, who was lying in the manger" (Luke 2:16).

PRAYER: *Lord Jesus, help us make a discovery. Help us discover the most important over the more important. We want to seek You over the celebration. In Your name we pray. Amen.*

THINK ABOUT THIS: The condition of the heart influences the traditions of the season.

—*Stan Toler*

Day 27

LUKE 2:17—
"When they had seen him,
they spread the word concerning what
had been told them about this child."

Humorist Dave Barry wrote,

To avoid offending anybody, the school dropped religion altogether and started singing about the weather. At my son's school, they now hold the winter program in February and sing increasingly non-memorable songs such as "Winter Wonderland," "Frosty the Snowman," and—this is a real song—"Suzy Snowflake," all of which is pretty funny because we live in Miami. A visitor from another planet would assume that the children belonged to the Church of Meteorology.[1]

True faith can't be concealed. It's like a hiccup. The more you try to keep it inside, the more likely it will be revealed. Our confused society may try to make His worship illegal, but the Savior will still be honored.

It may take the quiet Christmas carol of an elementary school child in a school cafeteria line or the defiant display of a manger scene on a small-town courthouse lawn. Somewhere and somehow, Christ will be seen. God intended it. "The Word became flesh and made his dwelling among us. We have seen his glory, the glory of the One and Only, who came from the Father, full of grace and truth" (John 1:14).

The shepherds were determined to be key witnesses. They didn't fully understand the message. They hadn't been schooled with the religious scholars of their day. They didn't have any idea what the implications of Christ's birth would mean on their society. They just knew they had to tell someone about their meeting Him.

The child of an atheist once asked, "Daddy, does God know we don't believe in Him?"

The question could be revised and asked of all of us at this season: "Does the world know that we believe in Him?"

We may have to put a manger scene instead of a Santa display on our front lawn. We may have to choose our Christmas cards for their message instead of their pretty pictures. We may have to express ourselves at a school board meeting called to debate taking all mention of Christ out of Christmas.

Whatever it takes, we must join the Judean shepherds in their determination to witness the marvelous gift of God that had just unfolded before their eyes.

However, we know something they didn't know. We know that this Child grew to sinless manhood and gave His own life for our salvation and holiness.

PRAYER: *Father, let me be bold to share Your Word with my world. In Your Son's name I pray. Amen.*

THINK ABOUT THIS: The secularization of Christmas begins with one careless heart.

—*Stan Toler*

Day 28

LUKE 2:19—
"Mary treasured up all these things and pondered them in her heart."

It's been said that renowned painter Leonardo da Vinci would sit for days reflecting on his projects. When painting his masterpiece *The Last Supper,* he spent hours in deep thought, waiting for the moment when the face of Christ would be revealed to him. He wanted just the right image in his mind to accurately portray the glory of the Christ. Anyone who has seen that great painting knows that the artist's time of reflection was worth every moment.

Selling materials for keepsakes and photo albums is now a multimillion-dollar business. Entire retail stores feature nothing but tools and supplies for memorabilia. And the concerns of those hobbyists focus on buying materials that will last.

Mary didn't have access to such supplies. She

stored the wonder of her Bethlehem days in a place where nothing would erode them—her heart.

The witness of the shepherds was just another thing for her to ponder. The angel's announcement, the birth of John the Baptist, Herod's threats, the journey to Bethlehem, the lack of space at the inn, the birth of her Baby in a manger cave—these awesome events called for a quiet time of reflection.

The Advent season is full of awesome events. But the heart that will know the love and the joy of the season will take time to reflect.

Travel agents today offer some unusual retreat packages. "One or two days in a monastery or a religious retreat center, away from the stress of the office or home, will be a time of refreshing," they say—and will only cost you $100 or $200.

We can save money and still enjoy those benefits by simply planning a daily time of reflection. Grab your Bible, journal, and a cup of coffee, and head for your spiritual retreat center. While you're there, take a side trip to Bethlehem. Go through your spiritual keepsakes and focus on the infinite love that God showed in the manger birth of His Son for your acceptance and forgiveness.

PRAYER: *Lord, forgive our busyness if it interferes with the spiritual business of knowing You better. Help us to take time to reflect on the sacrifice You made for our salvation and sanctification.*

THINK ABOUT THIS: Even the memories in our heart need a periodic dusting.

—*Stan Toler*

Day 29

LUKE 2:20—
"The shepherds returned, glorifying
and praising God for all the things
they had heard and seen."

Ethel Barrett, the great storyteller, once told about a little boy's letter to God:

Dear God,

I just started taking violin lessons. Please don't listen for a while, because I still squeak a lot.

Love,
Jimmy

The Bethlehem visitors didn't end their journey at the manger. That wasn't a place of endings—it was a place of beginnings. The hard part followed. They had to return to the loneliness of the desert—back to the sheep.

The wonder and the awe the shepherds had experienced now had to be fleshed out in their daily routine. It would have been nice to stay at Bethlehem. But the sheep needed a shepherd. They had to get on with their lives.

In one sense, they would always be the same. In another sense, they would never be the same. Their encounter with the Messiah child made every other experience pale in comparison. They had witnessed salvation come to earth. They had touched God.

All of us would like to stay a little longer at the manger. We don't care so much about the hurry and the scurry of the season. But we surely long to hang around the sacred for a little while longer.

But sheep need tending.

Classes need teaching. Sermons need preaching. Nails need hammering. Keyboards need typing. Houses need cleaning. We have to go back to the marketplace.

Yet, even there, we'll not be the same. We've just started taking "Bethlehem lessons." We still "squeak" a lot, but we're not the same as before. We learned how to glorify and praise God, but we'll have to keep working at it.

The Advent season isn't just about beginnings. It's about a victory walk that takes us and keeps us through the rough grind of the everyday.

Thank God for the journey. John Donne wrote about the One who accompanies us: "'Twas much that man was made like God before, / but that God should be like man much more."

So we'll keep practicing, even though we squeak a lot. And we'll keep trusting the One who invaded our times to take us victoriously to His eternity.

PRAYER: *Jesus, we need Your power and presence as we return to our homes or to the marketplace. We long to see You in this season, but we need to see You in every area of our daily lives as well. So may we glorify and praise You. In Your name we pray. Amen.*

THINK ABOUT THIS: Christmas is a one-day celebration, but it's a full-time application.

—*Stan Toler*

Day 30

MATTHEW 2:1-2—
"After Jesus was born in Bethlehem in
Judea, during the time of King Herod,
Magi from the east came to Jerusalem and
asked, 'Where is the one who has been
born king of the Jews? We saw his star in
the east and have come to worship him.'"

The visit of the magi is an interesting scenario in the early pages of the New Testament. There are a number of interesting things to consider here.

First, they were seekers. I like seekers—inquiring hearts, minds on a quest, searchers. Had they heard just enough about Jesus to whet their appetites? Had they gone with devious intent to destroy Jesus? Does it matter why they went? The fact that something happened while they were there is the important thing.

Second, they acknowledged Him as "king of the Jews" (2:2). Were they being polite? Naive? Again, it may not matter, but does it cast a hint on their searching?

Third, the real intent might have been to worship Him. Whatever their backgrounds, they might have felt the hunger and emptiness that even wise men without Christ feel. Church membership and denominational labels will not camouflage the heart's hunger. The human heart seeks reality and is restless and hungry until it finds the Christ.

Whatever we might suggest as reasons they came to worship Jesus, we know they sought Him and apparently found something—or Someone—who changed their lives. They "bowed down and worshiped him" (2:11).

Their journey had led them to Jesus, and their travel plans were changed. "Then they opened their treasures and presented him with gifts" (2:11). If we're to worship Him in truth, we must surrender our treasures and welcome Him as Lord. Such a surrender is the beginning of a deep and fulfilling journey with Jesus.

This is why wise men still seek Him.

PRAYER: *Father, give us seeking hearts today, that amid all the options we will seek You.*

THINK ON THIS: Many have found Jesus who were not seeking Him. Many are seeking but in the wrong places. Those who purposely seek Him are never disappointed.

—*C. Neil Strait*

An Advent Prayer

As we enter the season of Advent,
*   May we prepare our hearts for*
*   Your second Advent through self-examination.*

As we experience the season of Advent,
*   Let us find love, inspiration, and encouragement*
*   Through fellowship and worship together.*

As we reflect on the season of Advent,
*   Help us to recall the words of John 1:11-14,*
*   He came to that which was his own, but his own*
*   did not receive him.*
*   Yet to all who received him, to those who believed in*
*   his name, he gave the right to become children of*
*   God—children born not of natural descent, nor of*
*   human decision or a husband's will, but born of*
*   God. The Word became flesh and made his dwelling*
*   among us. We have seen his glory, the glory of the*
*   One and Only, who came from the Father, full of*
*   grace and truth.*
*   In the name of Jesus Christ we pray. Amen.*

—C. Neil Strait and Stan Toler

Notes

Day 6

1. C. H. Spurgeon, *The Treasury of David* (Grand Rapids: Baker Book House, 1977), 4:225.

Day 21

1. William Blaikie, *Manual of Bible History* (London: T. Nelson and Sons, 1906), 77.

Day 25

1. Charles Swindoll, *Growing Strong* (Grand Rapids: Zondervan Publishing House, 1994), 61.

Day 26

1. Taken from *The Tabernacle,* by Martin R. DeHaan. Copyright © 1955 by Zondervan Publishing House. Used by permission of Zondervan Publishing House.
2. Ibid.

Day 27

1. Dave Barry, "Notes on Western Civilization," *Chicago Tribune Magazine,* July 28, 1991, 29.